I0625362

Faith

Unlocking the Power of Faith: A Comprehensive Guide to Overcoming Obstacles, Achieving Success, and Finding Inner Peace in Your Personal and Professional Life - Transform Your Mindset, Boost Your Confidence, and Live Your Best Life Yet!

Lance P. Richards

Faith: Unlocking the Power of Faith: A Comprehensive Guide to Overcoming Obstacles, Achieving Success, and Finding Inner Peace in Your Personal and Professional Life - Transform Your Mindset, Boost Your Confidence, and Live Your Best Life Yet!

Table of Contents

01: Introduction: Why Faith Matters in Your Life

Faith is a fundamental aspect of human existence that has existed for thousands of years, providing individuals with a sense of purpose, direction, and hope. It is a concept that is often discussed in religious contexts, but faith extends beyond religion and can be applied to all aspects of life, including personal relationships, professional aspirations, and personal growth.

At its core, faith is about believing in something greater than oneself. It involves trust, confidence, and a willingness to surrender control to a higher power or purpose. This higher power can take many forms, including a divine being, a community, a cause, or simply a sense of inner strength.

Faith is essential because it provides us with a sense of meaning and purpose in life. When we have faith in something, we are motivated to pursue our goals and overcome obstacles, even when the path ahead seems challenging or uncertain. We are also more likely to persevere through difficult times because we have a belief that there is something greater waiting for us on the other side.

01: INTRODUCTION: WHY FAITH MATTERS IN YOUR LIFE

Moreover, faith provides us with a sense of inner peace and serenity. When we trust in a higher power or purpose, we are less likely to be consumed by worry, anxiety, or fear. Instead, we can find comfort in the knowledge that we are not alone and that there is a greater plan at work.

Faith also plays a significant role in personal and professional relationships. When we have faith in others, we are more likely to trust them and develop deeper, more meaningful connections. This trust and connection can lead to increased cooperation, collaboration, and mutual support, which are essential for success in both personal and professional contexts.

Furthermore, faith is essential for personal growth and development. When we have faith in ourselves, we are more likely to take risks, pursue new opportunities, and embrace change. This willingness to step outside of our comfort zone is necessary for personal growth and the attainment of our goals.

Overall, faith is a vital component of a fulfilling and meaningful life. It provides us with the strength, motivation, and inner peace necessary to overcome obstacles, achieve our goals, and find happiness and fulfillment in our personal and professional lives. Whether it is faith in a higher power, a community, a cause, or ourselves, we all have the ability to unlock the power of faith and live our best lives yet.

02: The Definition and Concept of Faith

Faith is a complex and multifaceted concept that has been the subject of debate and discussion for centuries. At its most basic level, faith can be defined as a belief or trust in something or someone that is unseen, unproven, or unknown. However, this definition only scratches the surface of what faith truly entails.

Faith can take many different forms, including religious faith, faith in oneself, faith in others, and faith in a cause or purpose. Religious faith, in particular, is perhaps the most well-known and widely practiced form of faith, with billions of people around the world placing their trust and belief in a higher power or divine being.

However, faith extends far beyond religion and can be found in all aspects of life. For example, faith in oneself involves believing in one's own abilities, potential, and worth. This type of faith is essential for personal growth, development, and success, as it provides the motivation and confidence necessary to pursue one's goals and overcome obstacles.

Faith in others involves trusting and believing in the people around us, including our friends, family, colleagues, and community members. This type of faith is essential for building strong, meaningful relationships, as it allows us to develop deeper connections based on trust, mutual respect, and support.

Faith in a cause or purpose involves believing in a larger mission or goal that goes beyond our individual selves. This type of faith is often found in social justice movements, environmental activism, and other similar causes that seek to make the world a better place.

Regardless of the form that faith takes, it is a powerful force that can transform our lives in profound ways. By placing our trust and belief in something greater than ourselves, we are able to find meaning, purpose, and direction in life.

However, faith is not without its challenges and obstacles. One of the biggest challenges of faith is dealing with doubt and uncertainty. When we place our trust in something that is unseen or unproven, it is natural to experience doubts and questions about the validity of our beliefs.

Moreover, faith can also be used as a tool for manipulation

and control, particularly in religious or spiritual contexts. It is essential to be mindful of these potential pitfalls and to approach faith with a critical, discerning eye.

Ultimately, the definition and concept of faith are complex and multifaceted, encompassing a wide range of beliefs, values, and practices. By understanding the different forms that faith can take and the challenges and obstacles that come with it, we can begin to unlock the true power of faith in our personal and professional lives.

03: Different Types of Faith

Faith comes in many different forms and can be expressed in a variety of ways. In this chapter, we will explore the various types of faith that exist and how they manifest in different areas of life.

– Religious Faith: Religious faith is perhaps the most well-known and widely practiced form of faith. It involves placing one's trust and belief in a higher power or divine being, such as God, Allah, or the Universe. Religious faith can take many different forms, including Christianity, Islam, Judaism, Hinduism, Buddhism, and many others. Religious faith often involves following a set of rituals, practices, and beliefs that are based on the teachings of a particular religion.

– Spiritual Faith: Spiritual faith is similar to religious faith in that it involves placing one's trust and belief in a higher power or divine force. However, spiritual faith is often more personal and individualized, and it may not be tied to any specific religion or set of beliefs. Spiritual faith can involve practices such as meditation, prayer, or mindfulness, and it may be focused on personal growth, self-awareness, and inner peace.

– Self-Faith: Self-faith involves placing one's trust and belief in oneself. This form of faith is essential for personal growth and development, as it provides the motivation and confidence necessary to pursue one's goals and overcome obstacles. Self-faith involves believing in one's own abilities, potential, and worth, and it can be strengthened through positive self-talk, setting and achieving goals, and seeking out opportunities for growth and learning.

– Interpersonal Faith: Interpersonal faith involves placing one's trust and belief in the people around us, including our friends, family, colleagues, and community members. This type of faith is essential for building strong, meaningful relationships, as it allows us to develop deeper connections based on trust, mutual respect, and support. Interpersonal faith can be strengthened through acts of kindness, communication, and active listening.

– Faith in a Cause or Purpose: Faith in a cause or purpose involves believing in a larger mission or goal that goes beyond our individual selves. This type of faith is often found in social justice movements, environmental activism, and other similar causes that seek to make the world a better place. Faith in a cause or purpose can be strengthened through education, awareness-raising, and active participation in social and political movements.

– Scientific Faith: Scientific faith involves placing one's trust and belief in the scientific method and the principles of evidence-based research. This type of faith is often associated with the natural sciences, such as physics, chemistry, and biology, and it involves using empirical data and experimentation to test and refine scientific theories. Scientific faith can be strengthened through critical thinking, skepticism, and a commitment to following the evidence wherever it leads.

– Creative Faith: Creative faith involves placing one's trust and belief in the power of creativity and the arts to transform and enrich our lives. This type of faith can take many different forms, including music, painting, writing, or performance art. Creative faith involves embracing the unknown and the unexpected, and it can be strengthened through experimentation, collaboration, and a willingness to take risks and try new things.

– Intellectual Faith: Intellectual faith involves placing one's trust and belief in the power of knowledge, education, and intellectual inquiry to solve problems and create positive change in the world. This type of faith can be found in many different fields, including science, philosophy, literature, and the humanities. Intellectual faith involves a commitment to lifelong learning, critical thinking, and a willingness to challenge and question established ideas and beliefs.

In conclusion, faith is a complex and multifaceted concept that can take many different forms. By understanding the different types of faith that exist and how they manifest in different areas of life, we can develop a more nuanced and holistic understanding of the role that faith plays in our personal and professional lives. Each type of faith brings its own unique benefits and challenges, and it is up to us to determine which forms of faith are most meaningful and relevant to our individual needs and goals.

Moreover, it is important to recognize that these different types of faith are not mutually exclusive, and many people may find themselves drawing upon multiple forms of faith in their daily lives. For example, someone may practice religious faith while also cultivating a strong sense of self-faith and interpersonal faith.

Overall, the different types of faith discussed in this chapter demonstrate that faith is a dynamic and complex concept that can be experienced in many different ways. By recognizing the diversity and richness of faith, we can develop a more inclusive and compassionate approach to understanding and supporting individuals from all walks of life. In the next chapter, we will explore how faith can help us overcome obstacles and achieve success in our personal and professional lives.

04: The Connection Between Faith and Religion

Faith and religion are two concepts that are often used interchangeably, but they are not necessarily the same thing. While religion can be seen as a formalized system of beliefs, practices, and traditions, faith is a more personal and individual experience that can exist outside of organized religion.

That being said, religion can be a powerful source of faith for many individuals. For those who practice a religion, faith is often a cornerstone of their beliefs and can help them find meaning, purpose, and comfort in their lives. Religious faith can provide a framework for understanding the world and one's place in it, as well as a sense of community and connection with others who share similar beliefs.

However, it is important to recognize that not everyone who has faith is religious, and not everyone who practices a religion has strong faith. There are many individuals who identify as spiritual but not religious, or who practice a religion but struggle with doubts or questions about their faith.

Regardless of whether one's faith is rooted in religion or

not, there are certain commonalities in how faith can impact one's life. Faith can provide a sense of hope, optimism,
and resilience in the face of adversity. It can also provide a
sense of purpose and direction, helping individuals to focus
on their goals and values.

Moreover, faith can also play a role in how individuals view
and interact with the world around them. For example,
some individuals may view the world through a lens of faith,
seeing their experiences and relationships as part of a larger, divine plan. Others may view their faith as a personal
journey of growth and self-discovery, seeking to connect
with something greater than themselves.

In addition to these more personal aspects of faith, there are
also social and cultural dimensions to religion that can impact individuals in a variety of ways. Religion can shape
one's identity, values, and sense of belonging, and can also
influence how individuals interact with others who do not
share their beliefs.

However, it is important to note that religion and faith can
also be a source of conflict and division, both within and
between communities. Religious differences have been at

the root of many conflicts throughout history, and even within a single religion, there may be different interpretations and beliefs that can cause tensions and disagreements.

Despite these potential challenges, faith and religion can also be a powerful force for unity, compassion, and social change. Many religious communities engage in charitable and social justice work, seeking to address issues such as poverty, inequality, and discrimination.

In conclusion, while faith and religion are not the same thing, they are closely related concepts that can have a significant impact on individuals and communities. Whether rooted in organized religion or not, faith can provide individuals with a sense of hope, purpose, and connection to something greater than themselves. However, it is important to approach faith with an open mind and a willingness to learn from and respect the beliefs and experiences of others.

05: The Power of Faith in Achieving Goals

Faith is a powerful tool for achieving goals in all aspects of life, whether personal or professional. When we have faith, we believe in ourselves and our ability to succeed, and we approach challenges with a positive and proactive mindset. Faith can help us stay focused on our goals, even when we face obstacles or setbacks, and can give us the strength and resilience to keep moving forward.

One of the key ways that faith can help us achieve our goals is by providing a sense of purpose and direction. When we have faith in ourselves and our abilities, we are more likely to set goals that align with our values and aspirations, and to take the necessary steps to achieve them. Faith can help us identify what we truly want out of life, and can motivate us to take action towards our dreams.

Another way that faith can support us in achieving our goals is by helping us overcome fear and self-doubt. When we have faith in ourselves and our abilities, we are less likely to be held back by feelings of insecurity or inadequacy. Instead, we are more likely to take risks and try new things, knowing that we have the strength and resilience to handle whatever challenges come our way.

In addition to these personal benefits, faith can also help us achieve our goals by connecting us with others who share our vision and values. Whether it's through a shared spiritual practice, a common interest or hobby, or a professional network, faith can help us build relationships with others who can support and encourage us in our goals. By working together towards a common purpose, we can achieve more than we could on our own.

Of course, having faith alone is not enough to achieve our goals. We also need to take concrete action towards our objectives, and be willing to put in the hard work and dedication required to make our dreams a reality. However, when we combine faith with action, we can create powerful momentum towards our goals and achieve results that may have once seemed impossible.

One important aspect of using faith to achieve goals is setting realistic expectations for ourselves. While faith can give us the confidence and optimism to pursue our dreams, we also need to be honest with ourselves about our abilities and limitations. Setting goals that are challenging but attainable can help us build momentum and gain confidence, while setting unrealistic goals can lead to disappointment and discouragement.

Another key factor in using faith to achieve goals is developing a growth mindset. Instead of seeing setbacks as failures, we can view them as opportunities for learning and growth. By embracing challenges and staying open to new experiences and perspectives, we can continue to build our faith and our abilities, and achieve even greater success in the future.

In conclusion, faith can be a powerful tool for achieving goals in all areas of life. By providing us with purpose, direction, and a positive mindset, faith can help us stay focused on our objectives and overcome obstacles along the way. Whether personal or professional, big or small, faith can help us achieve our goals and unlock our full potential.

06: The Benefits of a Faith-Filled Life

Living a faith-filled life can have numerous benefits for individuals in all aspects of their personal and professional lives. Faith can provide a sense of purpose and meaning, help individuals overcome challenges and adversity, promote positive relationships and connections, and foster a greater sense of inner peace and well-being.

One of the primary benefits of a faith-filled life is the sense of purpose and meaning it can provide. When individuals have a strong sense of faith, they are often guided by their beliefs and values, and are more likely to make decisions and take actions that align with their core principles. This can help individuals feel a greater sense of fulfillment and purpose in their lives, and can motivate them to pursue their goals and aspirations with greater passion and determination.

Faith can also help individuals overcome challenges and adversity. When faced with difficult situations, those with strong faith are often able to find comfort and solace in their beliefs, and may be more resilient in the face of adversity. This can help individuals maintain a positive outlook and attitude, even in difficult times, and can help them bounce back more quickly from setbacks and obstacles.

Another key benefit of a faith-filled life is the sense of community and connection it can provide. Many faith traditions involve gathering together with like-minded individuals to share experiences, offer support and encouragement, and build relationships. This can help individuals feel a sense of belonging and connectedness, and can promote positive social interactions and friendships.

Faith can also have positive impacts on mental and physical health. Research has shown that individuals who have a strong sense of faith may have lower levels of stress and anxiety, and may be less likely to experience depression and other mental health issues. In addition, those with a strong faith may be more likely to engage in healthy behaviors, such as regular exercise, healthy eating, and getting enough sleep, which can have positive impacts on physical health.

Finally, living a faith-filled life can help individuals find greater inner peace and well-being. By cultivating a sense of faith, individuals may be better able to find meaning and purpose in their lives, and may be more equipped to cope with stress and difficult situations. This can lead to a greater sense of overall well-being, and can help individuals feel more content and fulfilled in their lives.

In conclusion, there are numerous benefits to living a faith-filled life. From providing a sense of purpose and meaning, to helping individuals overcome challenges, build positive relationships, and find greater inner peace and well-being, faith can have a positive impact on individuals in all aspects of their lives. Whether through organized religion, personal spiritual practices, or other forms of faith, individuals who cultivate a strong sense of faith may find themselves better equipped to navigate the ups and downs of life, and to live their best lives yet.

07: Overcoming Obstacles through Faith

Faith is a powerful force that can help us overcome obstacles in our lives. Whether it's a personal or professional challenge, faith can give us the strength and courage to face difficult situations with a positive attitude and a sense of purpose. In this chapter, we will explore the different ways in which faith can help us overcome obstacles.

One of the primary ways in which faith can help us overcome obstacles is by providing us with hope. When we face a challenging situation, it's easy to become overwhelmed and feel like there's no way out. However, faith can give us the hope and optimism we need to keep going. We can trust that things will get better, and that we have the strength to overcome whatever challenges we're facing.

Faith can also provide us with a sense of purpose. When we're struggling with a difficult situation, it can be easy to lose sight of our goals and what we're working towards. However, faith can remind us of our purpose and why we're doing what we're doing. This can give us the motivation we need to keep moving forward, even when things are tough.

Another way in which faith can help us overcome obstacles is by providing us with a sense of community. When we're going through a difficult time, it's important to have people around us who support us and believe in us. Faith can provide us with a community of like-minded people who share our values and beliefs, and who can offer us support and encouragement when we need it most.

Faith can also help us to develop resilience. When we face obstacles and challenges, it can be easy to become discouraged and give up. However, faith can help us to develop the resilience we need to keep going, even when things are tough. We can draw on our faith to find the strength and courage we need to persevere through difficult times.

Finally, faith can help us to develop a positive mindset. When we're faced with obstacles and challenges, it's easy to fall into negative thinking patterns. However, faith can help us to cultivate a more positive outlook on life. We can focus on the things we're grateful for, and trust that things will work out in the end. This positive mindset can help us to overcome obstacles and achieve our goals.

In conclusion, faith can be a powerful tool for overcoming

obstacles in our lives. It can provide us with hope, purpose, community, resilience, and a positive mindset. By cultivating our faith, we can develop the strength and courage we need to face any challenge that comes our way.

08: Faith in Times of Crisis and Adversity

Introduction:

Life is not always easy, and we all go through challenging times that can shake us to our core. It could be a personal crisis like the loss of a loved one, a financial setback, or a health issue. Or it could be a global event that affects everyone, such as a pandemic, natural disaster, or war. No matter the nature of the adversity, it's normal to feel overwhelmed, anxious, or helpless. However, having faith can make all the difference in how we respond to these challenges. In this chapter, we'll explore how faith can help us navigate through difficult times and emerge stronger and more resilient.

The Power of Faith in Times of Crisis:

When we face a crisis, it's easy to feel alone and isolated, but having faith can give us a sense of connection and purpose. Faith is about trusting in a higher power, and this can provide comfort and solace during times of turmoil. Faith can also give us hope that things will get better, even when it seems impossible. This hope can sustain us and motivate us to keep moving forward, even when the path ahead is uncertain.

The Role of Faith Communities in Times of Crisis:

Faith communities can be a source of strength and support during difficult times. They provide a space for people to come together and share their experiences, fears, and hopes. Faith communities can also provide practical assistance, such as food, shelter, or financial aid, to those in need. In addition, faith communities often have rituals and traditions that can provide comfort and a sense of continuity during times of change and upheaval.

Faith as a Coping Mechanism:

Research has shown that faith can be a powerful coping mechanism during times of crisis. People who have a strong faith are often more resilient and better able to manage stress and anxiety. Faith can also help people find meaning and purpose in their suffering, which can make it easier to bear. Additionally, faith can provide a sense of control over the situation, even when the circumstances are beyond our control.

08: FAITH IN TIMES OF CRISIS AND ADVERSITY

The Dark Night of the Soul:

Despite the many benefits of faith, there are times when even the most devout believers may experience doubt, despair, or a crisis of faith. This is often referred to as the "dark night of the soul." It's a period of intense spiritual struggle, where we may question our beliefs, our purpose, and even the existence of a higher power. However, many faith traditions view this as a necessary part of the spiritual journey, and one that can ultimately lead to greater understanding and connection with the divine.

Overcoming Adversity Through Faith:

Faith can also help us overcome adversity and emerge stronger on the other side. When we face a crisis, it can be an opportunity for growth and transformation. By leaning on our faith, we can find the strength and courage to face our challenges head-on. We may also discover new aspects of ourselves, such as resilience, compassion, or creativity. In addition, going through a crisis can deepen our faith and strengthen our relationship with a higher power.

Conclusion:

08: FAITH IN TIMES OF CRISIS AND ADVERSITY

Faith can be a powerful tool for navigating through times of crisis and adversity. Whether we turn to faith for comfort, hope, or strength, it can help us find meaning and purpose in difficult times. Additionally, faith can provide a sense of connection and community, which is crucial for our emotional and spiritual well-being. Ultimately, faith can help us overcome obstacles and achieve our goals, both in our personal and professional lives.

09: Finding Inner Peace through Faith

Introduction

Faith is often considered a source of inner peace and comfort in times of distress. It can help individuals navigate life's challenges and find meaning and purpose even in difficult circumstances. In this chapter, we will explore how faith can help us find inner peace, what it means to be at peace with ourselves, and the ways in which faith can help us achieve this.

What is Inner Peace?

Inner peace can be described as a state of tranquility and harmony, a sense of calm and contentment with oneself and the world around us. It is a state of mind that allows us to accept our circumstances and let go of negative emotions, such as anger, anxiety, and fear. Inner peace is not the absence of problems or challenges, but rather the ability to cope with them in a calm and rational manner.

The Benefits of Inner Peace

Having inner peace has numerous benefits for our physical,

emotional, and mental well-being. Studies have shown that people who experience inner peace are less likely to suffer from stress-related illnesses, such as high blood pressure and heart disease. They are also more resilient and better able to cope with difficult situations. Inner peace also has a positive effect on our relationships, as it allows us to communicate more effectively and be more empathetic towards others.

How Faith Can Help Us Find Inner Peace

Faith can provide individuals with a sense of purpose and meaning in life. It can help us find a sense of inner peace and contentment by providing us with hope, guidance, and support. Through faith, we can develop a positive outlook on life and learn to see challenges as opportunities for growth and development. Faith can also provide us with a sense of community and belonging, which can be a source of comfort and support during difficult times.

The Role of Prayer and Meditation in Finding Inner Peace

Prayer and meditation are two practices that can help individuals find inner peace through faith. These practices allow us to quiet our minds and focus on our spiritual selves, which can help us find a sense of calm and tranquility. Prayer can also be a way to ask for guidance and strength during difficult times, while meditation can help us develop mindfulness and self-awareness.

Living a Faith-Filled Life

Living a faith-filled life involves more than just attending religious services or practicing prayer and meditation. It involves living in a way that aligns with our beliefs and values, treating others with kindness and compassion, and striving to be our best selves. Living a faith-filled life can bring us a sense of purpose and meaning, which can help us find inner peace and contentment.

Conclusion

Finding inner peace through faith is a journey that requires time, effort, and dedication. It involves developing a positive outlook on life, letting go of negative emotions, and striving to live in a way that aligns with our beliefs and values. Through prayer, meditation, and living a faith-filled life, we can find a sense of calm and tranquility even in the midst of life's challenges.

10: The Role of Faith in Personal Relationships

Faith plays a crucial role in personal relationships, whether it is with family, friends, or romantic partners. It is the foundation upon which trust, loyalty, and commitment are built. A lack of faith can lead to insecurity, doubt, and ultimately, the breakdown of relationships. In this chapter, we will explore the ways in which faith can enhance and strengthen personal relationships.

One of the key elements of a successful relationship is trust. Trust is built on the belief that the other person will do what they say they will do and will be honest with us. When we have faith in our partner, we are more likely to trust them. We believe that they have our best interests at heart and will act in ways that are consistent with our values and desires. This trust allows us to be vulnerable and open with our partner, which can deepen the emotional connection between us.

Another important aspect of faith in personal relationships is loyalty. When we have faith in someone, we are committed to them and their well-being. We are willing to stand by them through thick and thin, to support them when they need it, and to make sacrifices for their sake. Loyalty is a powerful force in relationships, as it creates a sense of security and stability that can help us weather difficult times together.

Faith can also help us to forgive and move on from past hurts in our relationships. When we have faith in our partner, we are more likely to believe that they are genuinely sorry for any wrongs they may have committed and that they are committed to making things right. This faith can make it easier for us to forgive them and to work towards healing our relationship.

Finally, faith can be a source of comfort and strength in times of difficulty. When we are facing challenges in our personal lives, having faith in our partner can help us to feel supported and cared for. We know that we are not alone and that we have someone who is rooting for us and cheering us on. This can give us the courage and strength we need to face our challenges and to come out on the other side stronger and more resilient.

In conclusion, faith is a vital ingredient in personal relationships. It provides the foundation for trust, loyalty, and com-

mitment, which are essential for healthy and thriving relationships. When we have faith in our partner, we can be vulnerable, forgiving, and supportive, which can deepen our
emotional connection and help us to weather the ups and
downs of life together.

11: The Role of Faith in Professional Relationships

Faith plays a significant role not only in personal relationships but also in professional relationships. In the workplace, faith can provide guidance, comfort, and strength to employees, as well as contribute to a positive work environment. Here are some ways faith can impact professional relationships:

– Establishing Common Values: Faith can create a shared set of values and beliefs among colleagues, regardless of their religious affiliations. When people share values such as honesty, integrity, and respect for others, it helps to foster trust and respect among colleagues.

– Providing a Sense of Purpose: Faith can provide a sense of purpose and meaning in one's work, beyond just earning a paycheck. When employees believe that their work has a greater purpose or is serving a higher cause, it can increase their motivation and job satisfaction.

– Encouraging Collaboration and Teamwork: Faith can encourage teamwork and collaboration by promoting the idea of serving others and working together towards a common goal. This can lead to more effective teamwork and a stronger sense of camaraderie among colleagues.

– Offering Support in Difficult Times: Faith can offer support and comfort to employees during difficult times, such as the loss of a loved one or a personal crisis. This support can help employees cope with stress and can strengthen their relationships with colleagues.

– Encouraging Ethical Behavior: Faith can encourage ethical behavior in the workplace by promoting values such as honesty, fairness, and compassion. When these values are integrated into the workplace culture, it can help to prevent unethical behavior and promote a positive work environment.

– Creating Opportunities for Service: Faith can provide opportunities for employees to serve others, whether it's through volunteering, charitable giving, or other forms of service. These opportunities can help employees feel more connected to their community and can contribute to a sense of purpose and fulfillment in their work.

– Promoting Respect and Tolerance: Faith can promote respect and tolerance for colleagues of different backgrounds and beliefs. When employees understand and appreciate each other's differences, it can lead to a more inclusive and diverse workplace.

It's important to note that while faith can have many positive effects on professional relationships, it's essential to respect everyone's individual beliefs and not impose one's faith on others. Colleagues should be free to express their beliefs, or lack thereof, without fear of judgment or discrimination.

In summary, faith can play a significant role in professional relationships by providing a shared set of values, a sense of purpose, support during difficult times, and promoting ethical behavior, respect, and tolerance. When integrated into the workplace culture, faith can help to create a positive work environment and contribute to the success of the organization.

12: Faith and Leadership

Leadership is the art of inspiring, influencing, and motivating people to work together to achieve a common goal. Faith can be a powerful tool for leaders to achieve success in their professional and personal lives. Faith in oneself and a higher power can help leaders overcome challenges, inspire their team, and create a positive impact on society. In this chapter, we will explore the role of faith in leadership, and how it can be used to achieve success and make a positive impact on the world.

Faith can help leaders develop a strong sense of purpose and direction. When leaders have faith in themselves and their abilities, they are more likely to set clear goals and pursue them with passion and determination. Faith can also help leaders develop a clear sense of their values and principles, which they can use to guide their decisions and actions.

Faith can also help leaders develop a strong sense of empathy and compassion. When leaders have faith in a higher power, they are more likely to see the world from a perspective of compassion and understanding. This can help leaders build stronger relationships with their team members, customers, and other stakeholders. It can also help leaders create a more inclusive and diverse workplace, where everyone feels valued and respected.

Faith can also help leaders overcome challenges and adversity. When leaders face difficult situations, their faith can give them the strength and courage to keep going. Faith can also help leaders see obstacles as opportunities for growth and learning, rather than as setbacks. This mindset can help leaders inspire their team members to overcome challenges and achieve their goals.

Faith can also help leaders create a positive impact on society. When leaders have faith in a higher power, they are more likely to be guided by a sense of purpose and a desire to make the world a better place. This can inspire leaders to create socially responsible businesses, support community projects, and engage in philanthropy. By leading with faith, leaders can inspire others to take action and create positive change in the world.

One example of a leader who used faith to achieve success and make a positive impact on society is Martin Luther King Jr. King was a Baptist minister who led the civil rights movement in the United States during the 1950s and 1960s. King's faith gave him the strength and courage to lead non-violent protests against racial discrimination and segregation. His leadership inspired millions of people around the world to stand up for justice and equality.

Another example of a leader who used faith to achieve success is Richard Branson. Branson is the founder of the Virgin Group, a multinational conglomerate with businesses in the travel, entertainment, and telecommunications industries. Branson has been open about his faith and how it has influenced his leadership style. In an interview with The Telegraph, Branson said, "My faith has helped me in business in the sense that it gives me a sense of perspective, and it helps me to treat people the way I would like to be treated."

In conclusion, faith can be a powerful tool for leaders to achieve success and make a positive impact on society. By having faith in oneself and a higher power, leaders can develop a strong sense of purpose, empathy, and resilience. They can also inspire their team members to overcome challenges and achieve their goals. By leading with faith, leaders can create businesses and communities that are inclusive, diverse, and socially responsible.

13: Faith and Resilience

Faith is a powerful force that can help us overcome adversity and build resilience in difficult times. Resilience is the ability to recover quickly from setbacks and adapt to new situations, and having faith can help us develop this ability.

When we face challenges in life, it can be easy to feel overwhelmed and lose hope. However, with faith, we can find strength and inspiration to keep moving forward. Faith can give us a sense of purpose and meaning, and it can help us see the bigger picture even when we're going through difficult times.

One way that faith can help us build resilience is by providing a sense of community and connection. Many religious and spiritual communities offer support and encouragement to their members, which can help us feel less isolated and more supported in times of crisis. Faith-based organizations may also offer practical resources, such as counseling or financial assistance, that can help us weather difficult times.

Another way that faith can help us build resilience is by providing a sense of inner peace and calm. When we have faith, we may feel a sense of trust and surrender to a higher power, which can help us let go of worry and anxiety. This doesn't mean that we ignore our problems or stop taking action to solve them, but rather that we approach them from a place of inner strength and calmness.

Faith can also help us cultivate a positive mindset that can contribute to resilience. When we have faith, we may believe that everything happens for a reason or that there is a greater purpose to our struggles. This perspective can help us find meaning and purpose in difficult situations, which can motivate us to keep going even when things get tough.

Additionally, faith can help us develop coping skills that can contribute to resilience. For example, prayer, meditation, and other spiritual practices can help us reduce stress and cultivate a sense of inner peace. These practices can also help us develop a greater sense of self-awareness and emotional regulation, which can help us navigate difficult emotions and situations more effectively.

It's important to note that building resilience through faith is not a one-size-fits-all approach. Different people may find different aspects of faith more helpful or relevant to their own experiences. Additionally, some people may find that their faith is challenged or even shaken by difficult experiences, which is a normal and natural part of the journey.

However, for those who find comfort, strength, and inspiration in their faith, it can be a powerful tool for building resilience and navigating difficult times. By cultivating a sense of community, inner peace, positive mindset, and coping skills, we can use our faith to help us weather life's storms and emerge stronger on the other side.

14: The Role of Faith in Mental Health

Introduction:

Faith can play a crucial role in maintaining and improving mental health. In this chapter, we will explore the ways in which faith can provide a source of comfort, hope, and strength for those who struggle with mental health issues. We will also discuss the importance of seeking professional help, in addition to relying on faith, in order to achieve optimal mental health.

The Connection between Faith and Mental Health:

Research has shown that there is a positive correlation between faith and mental health. For many people, faith provides a sense of purpose and meaning in life, which can be a powerful tool for coping with stress and adversity. Faith can also provide a source of social support, through participation in religious communities or by seeking guidance from religious leaders.

Studies have found that individuals who report a strong sense of religious or spiritual belief are less likely to experience symptoms of depression, anxiety, and other mental health disorders. This may be because faith can promote a positive outlook on life, encourage self-care practices, and provide a sense of hope for the future.

Additionally, for some people, faith can serve as a form of meditation or mindfulness practice, helping to reduce stress and anxiety by promoting a state of calm and inner peace.

The Importance of Professional Help:

While faith can be a powerful tool for promoting mental health, it is important to recognize that it is not a substitute for professional help. Mental health disorders are complex conditions that require specialized treatment and care.

In some cases, religious beliefs or practices may even contribute to mental health issues, particularly if they involve rigid or extreme beliefs that create feelings of guilt, shame, or isolation. For this reason, it is important to seek professional help if you are struggling with mental health issues, even if you are also relying on faith as a coping mechanism.

Working with a mental health professional can help you to identify and address the underlying causes of your mental

health issues, develop healthy coping strategies, and improve your overall quality of life.

Using Faith as a Tool for Coping with Mental Health Issues:

While professional help is essential for treating mental
health disorders, faith can still be a valuable tool for coping
with symptoms and promoting recovery. Here are some
ways that faith can be used as a tool for mental health:

– Find a supportive community: Participation in religious
communities can provide a source of social support and a
sense of belonging. If you are struggling with mental health
issues, seek out a community that is accepting and non-
judgmental.

– Practice self-care: Many religious practices involve self-
care practices, such as meditation, prayer, or fasting. These
practices can help to reduce stress and promote a sense of
calm.

– Find meaning and purpose: Faith can provide a sense of
purpose and meaning in life, which can be a powerful tool
for coping with stress and adversity. Focus on the aspects of
your faith that provide you with a sense of hope and direc-

tion.

– Seek guidance: Many religious leaders are trained to provide guidance and support to individuals struggling with mental health issues. Seek guidance from a trusted religious leader who can help you to navigate your mental health challenges.

Conclusion:

Faith can be a powerful tool for promoting mental health and wellbeing, providing a source of comfort, hope, and strength to those who struggle with mental health issues. However, it is important to recognize that faith is not a substitute for professional help. If you are struggling with mental health issues, it is important to seek the help of a mental health professional in addition to relying on faith as a coping mechanism. Together, faith and professional help can provide a comprehensive approach to mental health treatment and recovery.

15: The Role of Faith in Physical Health

Introduction:

Physical health is one of the essential aspects of our lives, and it is a foundation of our well-being. Without good physical health, it can be challenging to pursue our goals, live our best lives, and enjoy the world around us. Many factors can influence our physical health, including our lifestyle choices, genetics, environmental factors, and more. However, faith can also play a significant role in promoting physical health. In this chapter, we will explore the connection between faith and physical health, including how faith can impact our overall well-being and what we can do to strengthen our physical health through faith.

Faith and Physical Health:

There is a growing body of research that suggests a positive correlation between faith and physical health. According to a study published in the Journal of Religion and Health, individuals who practice faith tend to have better physical health outcomes, including a lower risk of heart disease, stroke, and cancer. Additionally, research has shown that faith-based interventions, such as prayer and meditation, can improve physical health outcomes in individuals with chronic conditions like asthma, hypertension, and diabetes.

One of the primary ways that faith can promote physical health is through stress reduction. Many of us experience stress in our daily lives, whether it's from work, relationships, or other sources. Chronic stress can have a negative impact on our physical health, leading to conditions such as high blood pressure, heart disease, and even mental health disorders like depression and anxiety. However, faith can provide a sense of comfort and support during difficult times, which can help reduce stress levels and promote overall physical health.

Faith can also encourage healthy lifestyle choices, such as regular exercise, healthy eating, and avoiding risky behaviors like smoking and excessive alcohol consumption. For example, many faith-based communities offer opportunities for physical activity, such as sports teams, exercise classes, and outdoor activities. Additionally, faith-based teachings often promote healthy behaviors, such as moderation and self-care, which can promote physical health and well-being.

Finally, faith can provide a sense of purpose and meaning, which can be essential for maintaining good physical health. Research has shown that individuals who have a sense of purpose in life tend to have better physical health outcomes, including a lower risk of chronic conditions like heart disease and diabetes. Faith can provide a sense of purpose and meaning by promoting values like compassion, empathy, and service to others, which can help individuals feel a sense of fulfillment and satisfaction in their lives.

Practical Tips for Strengthening Physical Health through Faith:

If you are interested in strengthening your physical health through faith, there are several practical tips you can follow:

– Make physical activity a regular part of your faith practice. Consider joining a faith-based sports team, exercise class, or outdoor activity group.

– Use faith-based teachings to guide healthy lifestyle choices, such as eating a balanced diet, getting enough sleep, and avoiding risky behaviors like smoking and excessive alcohol consumption.

– Practice stress-reducing techniques like prayer, meditation, and deep breathing exercises.

– Seek out opportunities for service to others, such as volunteering at a local charity or helping those in need in your community.

– Connect with others who share your faith and are committed to promoting physical health and well-being.

Conclusion:

Physical health is an essential aspect of our overall well-being, and faith can play a significant role in promoting good physical health. By reducing stress, promoting healthy lifestyle choices, and providing a sense of purpose and meaning, faith can help individuals maintain good physical health and enjoy a higher quality of life. If you are interested in strengthening your physical health through faith, consider incorporating these practical tips into your daily routine and seeking out opportunities for connection and service within your faith community.

16: The Intersection of Faith and Science

Faith and science are often seen as two opposing forces, but they do not have to be mutually exclusive. In fact, many scientists have found that faith and science can work together to provide a greater understanding of the world around us. This chapter explores the intersection of faith and science, and how they can work together to provide a more complete view of the world.

At its core, faith is about belief in things that cannot be proven by science. This includes belief in a higher power, the afterlife, and the soul. While science may not be able to prove the existence of these things, it can help us understand the world in which we live. For example, science can help us understand the complex processes that go on in the natural world, including the development of life on Earth and the structure of the universe.

Science has also helped us understand the role of spirituality and faith in our mental and physical health. Studies have shown that faith and spirituality can have a positive impact on mental health, including reducing symptoms of depression and anxiety, improving overall well-being, and increasing resilience in the face of stress and adversity.

In terms of physical health, studies have shown that religious individuals tend to have lower rates of substance abuse, obesity, and high blood pressure. There is also evidence to suggest that faith and spirituality can help individuals cope with chronic illnesses, such as cancer, and even improve outcomes in some cases.

While science and faith may seem to be at odds with one another, they can work together to provide a more complete understanding of the world. For example, science can help us understand how the brain processes spiritual experiences, while faith can provide a deeper understanding of the meaning behind those experiences.

Additionally, the principles of science and faith can complement one another. Both require a level of curiosity and inquiry, a willingness to explore the unknown, and a desire to understand the world in a deeper way. Both also require humility, recognizing that there is always more to learn and discover.

One example of how science and faith can work together is the study of the origin of the universe. While science can explain how the universe came into being through the Big Bang, faith can provide a deeper understanding of the meaning and purpose behind the creation of the universe.

Another example is the study of the human mind. While science can help us understand the underlying neurological processes that give rise to consciousness and awareness, faith can provide a deeper understanding of the nature of the soul and the spiritual aspect of human existence.

In conclusion, the intersection of faith and science is a complex and often misunderstood area. While they may seem to be at odds with one another, they can work together to provide a more complete understanding of the world around us. By embracing both faith and science, individuals can gain a deeper understanding of themselves, their place in the world, and the nature of existence itself.

17: Faith and Community Building

Introduction:

In today's world, the importance of community building cannot be overstated. People need a sense of belonging and connection to thrive, and communities play a significant role in providing that. Faith-based communities, in particular, can be a powerful force for building connections and supporting individuals and families. In this chapter, we will explore the ways in which faith can contribute to community building and how communities can be strengthened by faith-based practices.

Faith-Based Communities:

Faith-based communities, whether they are centered around a particular religion or not, often serve as the backbone of a community. They provide a sense of stability and continuity, as well as a framework for shared beliefs and values. Faith communities also tend to be more cohesive, as members share a common purpose and mission.

At the heart of faith-based communities is the belief in something greater than oneself. This belief can create a sense of humility and service, as individuals seek to serve their higher power and their fellow community members. It can also lead to a sense of responsibility and stewardship, as members seek to care for the world around them.

Faith-Based Practices:

Many faith-based practices can contribute to community building. One of the most important is the practice of worship. Worship brings people together in a shared experience, allowing them to connect with one another and their higher power. This shared experience can be powerful, creating a sense of unity and belonging.

Another important faith-based practice is service. Many faiths place a strong emphasis on serving others, whether through volunteer work, charitable giving, or other means. This service can be a powerful way to build community, as individuals come together to support a common cause and work towards a shared goal.

Finally, faith-based communities often prioritize education and learning. Many offer classes and other educational opportunities, allowing members to deepen their knowledge and understanding of their faith. This shared learning experience can be another powerful way to build community, as individuals come together to learn and grow.

Building Bridges:

Faith-based communities can also be powerful bridges between different groups. They can serve as a place where people of different races, cultures, and backgrounds can come together in a shared experience. This can be particularly important in today's divided world, where it can be difficult to find common ground.

In addition, faith-based communities can also serve as a place where individuals who have experienced trauma or hardship can find support and healing. Many faiths place a strong emphasis on compassion and empathy, and members of these communities may be more likely to extend a helping hand to those in need.

Conclusion:

Faith-based communities have the potential to be powerful forces for community building. They provide a framework for shared beliefs and values, and they can bring people together in a shared experience. By prioritizing service, education, and worship, faith-based communities can create a sense of belonging and connection that is essential for personal and communal well-being. Additionally, they can serve as bridges between different groups and provide support and healing for those in need. In a world where divisions seem to be growing, faith-based communities offer a path towards greater unity and connection.

18: The Role of Faith in Social Justice

Introduction

Faith has played a significant role in social justice movements throughout history. From the Civil Rights Movement to the Women's Suffrage Movement, people of faith have been at the forefront of advocating for equality and justice for all. In this chapter, we will explore the role of faith in social justice and how it can be a powerful force for positive change in our society.

The Relationship Between Faith and Social Justice

Faith and social justice have a strong relationship because many faith traditions teach values that align with the principles of social justice. For example, the Abrahamic religions (Judaism, Christianity, and Islam) teach the importance of treating others with respect, dignity, and compassion. The concept of justice is also central to these religions, as they believe in a just and fair God who holds people accountable for their actions.

In addition, many faith communities have a long history of

advocacy and social justice work. For example, the Civil Rights Movement in the United States was largely led by African American churches, with leaders like Martin Luther King Jr. drawing on their faith to inspire and motivate others to fight for justice and equality.

Faith-based organizations and charities also play a crucial role in addressing social issues. Many of these organizations work to alleviate poverty, provide access to education and healthcare, and promote human rights and dignity for all people.

Examples of Faith-Based Social Justice Movements

Throughout history, faith-based movements have played a critical role in promoting social justice. Here are some examples:

The Civil Rights Movement: The Civil Rights Movement was a social movement in the United States during the 1950s and 1960s that aimed to end racial segregation and discrimination against African Americans. Many of the leaders of the movement, such as Martin Luther King Jr. and Rosa Parks, were inspired by their faith to fight for justice and equality.

18: THE ROLE OF FAITH IN SOCIAL JUSTICE

The Women's Suffrage Movement: The Women's Suffrage Movement was a social movement in the late 19th and early 20th centuries that aimed to secure voting rights for women. Many of the leaders of the movement were motivated by their faith to fight for gender equality.

The Anti-Apartheid Movement: The Anti-Apartheid Movement was a social movement in South Africa and other countries that aimed to end the system of racial segregation and discrimination known as apartheid. Many religious leaders, including Archbishop Desmond Tutu, played a key role in the movement.

Faith and Social Justice Today

Today, faith-based organizations and communities continue to play a critical role in social justice movements. Many faith communities are actively engaged in promoting social justice issues such as climate change, immigration reform, and income inequality.

One example of a faith-based organization working for social justice today is the Catholic Campaign for Human Development, which works to address poverty in the United States through community organizing and economic development programs.

Another example is the Muslim Advocates organization, which works to promote justice and equality for American Muslims and to fight against discrimination and hate crimes.

Conclusion

Faith has played and continues to play a critical role in social justice movements. Faith communities and organizations bring unique strengths and perspectives to these movements, and their values and beliefs can inspire and motivate people to work for a more just and equitable society. By working together, people of all faiths and backgrounds can make significant progress towards a more just and equitable world.

19: The Role of Faith in Forgiveness

Introduction:

Forgiveness is an act of compassion, and it is an essential aspect of our spiritual and emotional wellbeing. It is often easy to hold grudges and keep the anger and pain of the past with us, but forgiveness offers a path to move on from the pain and hurt, and it has the power to heal relationships and transform our lives. In this chapter, we will explore the role of faith in forgiveness, the benefits of forgiveness, and how we can practice forgiveness in our lives.

Faith and Forgiveness:

Forgiveness is a central tenet of many faiths, including Christianity, Judaism, Islam, Buddhism, and Hinduism. In the Christian tradition, forgiveness is emphasized in the Lord's Prayer, where Jesus teaches his disciples to ask God to "forgive us our trespasses, as we forgive those who trespass against us." Forgiveness is also a central message in the teachings of Buddha, who emphasized the importance of letting go of anger and resentment to achieve inner peace.

The Role of Forgiveness in Our Lives:

Forgiveness has many benefits for our emotional, spiritual, and physical health. When we forgive others, we let go of the anger and pain that we hold within us, and we can move forward with our lives. Forgiveness can also help to heal relationships that have been damaged by hurt and betrayal, and it can bring us closer to those we love. Forgiveness can also help to reduce stress and anxiety, and it can lead to better physical health.

How to Practice Forgiveness:

Practicing forgiveness can be difficult, especially when we have been hurt deeply by someone we love. However, forgiveness is a choice that we can make, and it is a process that we can learn. Here are some steps that we can take to practice forgiveness in our lives:

– Acknowledge the Pain: The first step in forgiveness is to acknowledge the pain that we feel. We need to be honest with ourselves about the hurt and anger that we are experiencing, and we need to be willing to feel these emotions fully.

– Choose to Forgive: Forgiveness is a choice that we make, and we need to be willing to let go of our anger and resentment. We need to choose to forgive the person who has hurt us, even if we do not feel like it.

– Release the Anger: Forgiveness involves releasing the anger and resentment that we feel towards the person who has hurt us. We can do this by journaling, talking to a trusted friend or therapist, or practicing mindfulness meditation.

– Practice Empathy: It can be helpful to try to understand the perspective of the person who has hurt us. By putting ourselves in their shoes, we can gain a deeper understanding of their actions and motivations, which can make it easier to forgive them.

– Let Go of Resentment: Forgiveness involves letting go of the resentment and bitterness that we feel towards the person who has hurt us. We can do this by focusing on the present moment, practicing gratitude, and cultivating a positive attitude.

Conclusion:

Forgiveness is an essential aspect of our emotional and spiritual wellbeing, and it has the power to transform our lives. By practicing forgiveness, we can let go of the pain and anger that we hold within us, and we can move forward with our lives. Faith can be a powerful tool in our journey towards forgiveness, as it offers us the strength and courage to choose compassion and kindness, even in the face of hurt and betrayal. By choosing to forgive, we can find peace, healing, and freedom, and we can live our best lives yet.

20: The Role of Faith in Overcoming Addiction

Introduction:

Addiction is a serious problem that affects millions of people worldwide. It can manifest in various forms, including drug addiction, alcoholism, gambling addiction, and others. Addiction can have severe consequences on an individual's physical and mental health, personal relationships, and professional life. It is a complex condition that requires a multifaceted approach to treatment.

One approach that has shown promising results in overcoming addiction is faith-based treatment. Faith-based treatment incorporates the teachings and principles of various religions and spiritual practices to help individuals overcome addiction. This chapter will explore the role of faith in overcoming addiction and how it can help individuals achieve long-term recovery.

Faith-Based Treatment:

Faith-based treatment is an approach to addiction treatment that involves integrating religious or spiritual practices into the recovery process. It can be helpful for individuals who have a strong religious or spiritual foundation or those who are open to exploring the role of faith in their recovery journey.

Faith-based treatment can take various forms, depending on the individual's religious or spiritual beliefs. For example, some faith-based treatment programs incorporate prayer, meditation, and reading religious texts into their recovery program. Others may include group discussions or counseling sessions that explore the spiritual and emotional aspects of addiction and recovery.

The Role of Faith in Overcoming Addiction:

Faith can play a vital role in overcoming addiction by providing individuals with a sense of purpose, hope, and support. It can help individuals develop a stronger sense of self and a more profound connection to their values and beliefs. Here are some ways faith can help individuals overcome addiction:

– Finding Purpose and Meaning:

Addiction can leave individuals feeling lost and without a

sense of purpose. Faith can help individuals find meaning in their lives and provide a sense of purpose. It can also help individuals connect with a higher power and feel a sense of belonging to a greater community.

– Providing Hope:

Addiction can make individuals feel hopeless and helpless. Faith can provide hope and encourage individuals to believe that recovery is possible. It can also provide individuals with the strength and motivation to overcome the challenges of addiction.

– Offering Support:

Faith-based communities can offer individuals a supportive network of people who understand the challenges of addiction and recovery. These communities can provide emotional, spiritual, and practical support to help individuals overcome addiction and achieve long-term recovery.

– Developing Self-Awareness:

Faith can help individuals develop a deeper understanding of themselves and their values. This self-awareness can be helpful in identifying triggers and underlying issues that contribute to addiction. It can also help individuals develop a stronger sense of self-control and resilience.

– Promoting Forgiveness:

Addiction can create feelings of guilt, shame, and regret. Faith can help individuals learn to forgive themselves and others and move forward in their recovery journey.

Challenges of Faith-Based Treatment:

While faith-based treatment can be effective for some individuals, it may not be suitable for everyone. Some challenges of faith-based treatment include:

– Not everyone has a strong religious or spiritual foundation.

– Some individuals may feel uncomfortable discussing their beliefs in group settings.

– Some individuals may feel excluded if they do not share the same religious or spiritual beliefs as others in the group.

– Some individuals may have negative experiences associated with religion or spirituality, which may hinder their willingness to engage in faith-based treatment.

Conclusion:

Faith-based treatment can be a valuable tool in overcoming addiction. It can provide individuals with a sense of purpose, hope, and support to help them achieve long-term recovery. However, it may not be suitable for everyone, and individuals should explore various treatment options to find the approach that works best for them. With the right support and resources, individuals can overcome addiction and achieve a happier, healthier, and more fulfilling life.

21: Faith and Self-Reflection

Self-reflection is the process of examining our thoughts, feelings, and actions to gain a deeper understanding of ourselves. It allows us to identify our strengths and weaknesses, recognize areas for growth and improvement, and develop a sense of self-awareness. In today's fast-paced world, self-reflection is becoming increasingly important for personal and professional development. However, self-reflection can be a daunting task for many of us, especially when we are confronted with our own flaws and shortcomings.

In this chapter, we will explore the role of faith in self-reflection. Faith can provide us with the courage, strength, and guidance to examine ourselves honestly and to make positive changes in our lives. We will discuss how faith can help us overcome the fear and resistance that often prevent us from engaging in self-reflection. We will also examine how faith can provide us with a sense of purpose and meaning, which can help us navigate the challenges of self-reflection and personal growth.

Self-reflection can be a challenging and uncomfortable process. It requires us to confront our own weaknesses, vulnerabilities, and mistakes. For many of us, this can be a frightening prospect. We may fear that if we look too closely at ourselves, we will discover something we don't like, or that we will be judged or rejected by others.

This fear can be especially strong when we are confronting issues related to our faith. We may fear that if we question our beliefs or values, we will lose our connection to God or our religious community. We may also fear that if we acknowledge our doubts or uncertainties, we will be seen as weak or unfaithful.

However, it is important to remember that self-reflection is not about judging or condemning ourselves. It is about gaining a deeper understanding of ourselves and recognizing areas where we can grow and improve. Faith can provide us with the courage and strength to confront our fears and to engage in self-reflection with honesty and openness.

Faith can also provide us with a sense of self-awareness. When we have a strong faith, we have a clear understanding of our values, beliefs, and priorities. This can help us make decisions that are aligned with our sense of purpose and meaning, and can help us navigate the challenges of self-reflection and personal growth.

For example, if we believe that kindness and compassion are important values, we can use these values as a guide for our self-reflection. We can examine our thoughts, feelings, and actions to see if they are aligned with these values, and make changes if necessary. This can help us develop a greater sense of self-awareness and can lead to personal growth and development.

Faith can also provide us with a sense of perspective. When we have a strong faith, we understand that we are part of something larger than ourselves. We may believe that we are part of a divine plan, or that our lives have a purpose that is greater than our individual desires or ambitions. This can help us maintain a sense of humility and perspective, even as we engage in the sometimes difficult process of self-reflection.

Self-reflection can also involve confronting past mistakes and failures. This can be a painful process, and it can be difficult to forgive ourselves for the mistakes we have made. However, faith can provide us with the power of forgiveness.

Many religious traditions emphasize the importance of forgiveness, both of ourselves and of others. For example, in Christianity, forgiveness is central to the teachings of Jesus, who taught his followers to "love your enemies and pray for those who persecute you" (Matthew 5:44). The practice of confession and absolution can also be a powerful tool for self-forgiveness and healing.

Self-reflection is a critical component of personal growth and development. It is the process of introspection, where we take a step back and examine our thoughts, emotions, and actions. By reflecting on our experiences, we gain a better understanding of ourselves, our strengths and weaknesses, and our values and beliefs.

Faith plays a significant role in self-reflection, as it provides a framework for understanding ourselves and our place in the world. When we have faith, we believe in something greater than ourselves, and this belief can help us make sense of our experiences and find meaning in our lives.

One way that faith can aid in self-reflection is by providing a sense of purpose. When we have a sense of purpose, we are more likely to engage in self-reflection because we are motivated to improve ourselves and our lives. Faith can provide this sense of purpose by helping us to understand our place in the world and our role in a larger plan.

Faith can also provide a sense of guidance and direction in our self-reflection. When we are struggling with a problem or trying to make an important decision, we can turn to our faith for guidance. Our faith can provide us with a set of values and principles that we can use to guide our actions and decisions.

Additionally, faith can help us to stay grounded and centered during our self-reflection. When we engage in self-reflection, it can be easy to become overwhelmed by our thoughts and emotions. However, faith can help us to remain focused and calm during this process. By turning to our faith, we can find peace and clarity in our reflections.

Moreover, faith can also help us to cultivate self-compassion during our self-reflection. When we reflect on our past actions or mistakes, it can be easy to be overly critical of ourselves. However, faith teaches us that we are all imperfect and that we can find forgiveness and redemption through our beliefs. By incorporating our faith into our self-reflection, we can cultivate a sense of self-compassion and learn to be kinder to ourselves.

In conclusion, self-reflection is a critical component of personal growth and development, and faith can play a significant role in this process. By providing a sense of purpose, guidance, and direction, helping us to stay grounded and centered, and cultivating self-compassion, faith can aid us in our self-reflection and help us to become the best versions of ourselves.

22: Faith and Self-Awareness

Introduction

Faith can be a powerful tool for self-awareness. It allows individuals to connect with their inner selves, their beliefs, and their values. When we have faith, we have a sense of purpose and direction, and this can help us to become more self-aware. In this chapter, we will explore how faith can enhance our self-awareness and how we can use it as a tool for personal growth.

What is self-awareness?

Self-awareness is the ability to recognize and understand one's own thoughts, feelings, and behaviors. It involves taking an honest and objective look at oneself, including one's strengths, weaknesses, and motivations. Self-awareness is a crucial aspect of personal growth, as it enables us to identify areas for improvement and develop strategies for self-improvement.

The Connection Between Faith and Self-Awareness

Faith can help us to become more self-aware by providing us with a framework for understanding ourselves and the world around us. When we have faith, we have a set of be-liefs and values that guide our thoughts and actions. These beliefs and values can help us to understand ourselves bet-ter and to recognize our strengths and weaknesses.

Faith also provides us with a sense of purpose and direc-tion. When we have faith, we have a reason for living, and this can help us to focus on what is important and to make decisions that align with our values. This clarity of purpose can also help us to identify areas for improvement and to set goals for personal growth.

Faith can also help us to become more self-aware by provid-ing us with a sense of perspective. When we have faith, we believe in something greater than ourselves, and this can help us to see our problems and challenges in a broader context. This broader perspective can help us to identify the root causes of our problems and to develop strategies for overcoming them.

How to Use Faith for Self-Awareness

Here are some ways in which you can use faith as a tool for self-awareness:

– Identify Your Beliefs and Values

To use faith as a tool for self-awareness, it is essential to identify your beliefs and values. Take some time to reflect on what is important to you, what you believe in, and what you stand for. Write down your beliefs and values, and use them as a guide for your thoughts and actions.

– Develop a Practice of Reflection and Meditation

Reflection and meditation are powerful tools for self-awareness. They can help you to become more in tune with your thoughts and feelings, and to develop a deeper understanding of yourself. Set aside some time each day for reflection and meditation, and use this time to connect with your inner self.

– Practice Mindfulness

Mindfulness is the practice of being present in the moment and paying attention to your thoughts and feelings without judgment. Mindfulness can help you to become more self-aware by helping you to identify your thoughts and feelings as they arise. Practice mindfulness throughout the day, and use it as a tool for self-reflection.

22: FAITH AND SELF-AWARENESS

– Seek Guidance and Support from Your Faith Community

Your faith community can be a valuable source of guidance and support for self-awareness. Seek out mentors, counselors, and other members of your faith community who can help you to deepen your understanding of yourself and your faith.

– Set Goals for Personal Growth

Use your faith as a guide for setting goals for personal growth. Identify areas where you would like to improve, and develop strategies for achieving your goals. Use your beliefs and values as a guide for your personal growth, and stay connected to your faith community for guidance and support.

One way to enhance self-awareness through faith is through meditation and prayer. These practices encourage individuals to reflect on their thoughts, emotions, and actions, and to be present in the moment. This can help them gain insight into their values, beliefs, and behaviors, and to identify areas where they may need to make changes.

Additionally, faith can provide individuals with a sense of

purpose and direction, which can enhance self-awareness. When individuals have a clear understanding of their values and beliefs, they are better able to make decisions that align with their goals and aspirations. They are also better able to identify their strengths and weaknesses and to take actions to improve themselves.

Moreover, faith can provide a sense of connection to something greater than oneself, which can enhance self-awareness. When individuals feel connected to a higher power or a community of believers, they may be more likely to view themselves as part of a larger whole, and to consider how their thoughts and actions impact others.

In addition to meditation and prayer, other practices that can enhance self-awareness through faith include journaling, attending religious services or retreats, and engaging in spiritual practices such as fasting or charitable giving. These practices encourage individuals to reflect on their beliefs and values, to identify areas where they may need to make changes, and to develop a deeper understanding of themselves and their place in the world.

Overall, faith can play a significant role in enhancing self-awareness, by encouraging individuals to reflect on their thoughts, emotions, and actions, to gain insight into their values and beliefs, and to develop a sense of connection to something greater than oneself. By developing a greater understanding of themselves and their place in the world, individuals can cultivate greater self-awareness, which can lead to greater success and fulfillment in their personal and professional lives.

23: The Importance of Faith in Decision-Making

Introduction

Life is a continuous process of decision-making. We make decisions every day, from what to wear, what to eat, where to go, and who to spend our time with. We also make bigger decisions that affect our lives, such as choosing a career path, starting a business, or getting married. These decisions can be daunting and overwhelming, and it is essential to have a solid foundation to guide us in making the right choices. In this chapter, we will explore the importance of faith in decision-making and how it can help us navigate life's challenges.

The Role of Faith in Decision-Making

Faith plays a critical role in decision-making. It provides us with a sense of purpose and direction, helping us to align our choices with our beliefs and values. Faith can help us to see beyond our present circumstances and envision a better future. It gives us hope and optimism, even in the face of uncertainty.

23: THE IMPORTANCE OF FAITH IN DECISION-MAKING

Making decisions based on faith involves trusting in a higher power and surrendering control. It requires us to listen to our inner voice and seek guidance from our faith community. Faith encourages us to seek wisdom and knowledge from spiritual leaders and texts, as well as from trusted mentors and advisors.

Faith-based decision-making can also help us to make decisions that are in the best interest of ourselves and others. It teaches us to consider the impact of our choices on those around us and to act with compassion and empathy.

Faith and Decision-Making in Practice

In practice, making decisions based on faith involves taking time for self-reflection and prayer. It requires us to seek guidance from our faith community and to be open to the advice and support of others. It also involves being mindful of our thoughts and actions, and staying true to our values and beliefs.

One way to incorporate faith into decision-making is to create a decision-making framework based on spiritual principles. This framework can help us to make decisions that align with our faith and values. For example, if honesty and integrity are important values, we can make decisions that prioritize these principles. If compassion and empathy are important, we can make decisions that reflect these values.

Faith can also help us to overcome fear and uncertainty in decision-making. When we have faith, we can trust that things will work out for the best, even if the outcome is not what we initially wanted. We can let go of our fears and doubts, and take bold steps towards our goals.

The Benefits of Faith-Based Decision-Making

Making decisions based on faith can have numerous benefits. It can provide us with a sense of peace and calm, knowing that we are making choices that are in line with our beliefs and values. It can also give us clarity and focus, helping us to prioritize our goals and stay on track. Faith-based decision-making can also lead to greater confidence and self-esteem, as we learn to trust in our abilities and the guidance of our higher power.

Moreover, faith-based decision-making can help us to develop resilience and adaptability. When we trust in a higher power, we can overcome obstacles and setbacks with a greater sense of purpose and optimism. We can learn from our mistakes and use them as opportunities for growth and self-improvement.

Conclusion

Faith plays a critical role in decision-making. It provides us with a solid foundation to guide us in making the right choices, aligning our decisions with our beliefs and values. By incorporating faith into our decision-making process, we can cultivate a sense of peace, purpose, and direction, even in the face of uncertainty. We can also develop resilience and adaptability, learning from our mistakes and using them as opportunities for growth and self-improvement. Ultimately, faith-based decision-making can help us to live a fulfilling and meaningful life, achieving our goals and realizing our full potential.

24: Faith and Goal-Setting

Introduction:

Have you ever felt like you were stuck in a rut, unable to move forward in your personal or professional life? Maybe you've set goals for yourself but you haven't been able to achieve them. Or maybe you're not sure what your goals are and you feel lost and directionless. Whatever the case may be, having faith can be the key to unlocking the power to overcome obstacles, achieve success, and find inner peace.

In this chapter, we'll explore the connection between faith and goal-setting. We'll look at how having faith can help you set and achieve your goals, and we'll provide practical tips and strategies for incorporating faith into your goal-setting process. Whether you're just starting out on your goal-setting journey or you're looking to take your goal-setting to the next level, this chapter will help you tap into the power of faith to achieve your dreams.

The Power of Faith:

Faith is a powerful force that can transform your life in countless ways. When you have faith, you believe that anything is possible. You trust that there is a higher power at work in the universe, guiding you toward your purpose and helping you overcome obstacles along the way.

Having faith can give you the strength and courage you need to pursue your goals, even when the road ahead seems daunting. It can help you stay focused and motivated, even when you encounter setbacks or obstacles. And it can provide a sense of inner peace and fulfillment that can't be found through material possessions or external achievements.

When it comes to goal-setting, having faith can make all the difference. Without faith, it's easy to get discouraged when things don't go as planned. But with faith, you can trust that everything happens for a reason and that there is a higher purpose behind every obstacle you encounter.

Setting Goals with Faith:

So how can you incorporate faith into your goal-setting process? Here are some practical tips and strategies:

– Start with prayer or meditation: Before you even begin setting your goals, take some time to connect with your higher power through prayer or meditation. Ask for guidance and clarity as you set your goals, and trust that you will receive the answers you need.

– Visualize your goals: Use your imagination to visualize what your life will look like once you've achieved your goals. Imagine yourself living your dream life, and feel the emotions that come with it. This can help you stay motivated and focused as you work toward your goals.

– Write down your goals: Studies show that people who write down their goals are more likely to achieve them. Write down your goals in a journal or on a piece of paper, and review them regularly to stay focused and motivated.

– Break your goals down into smaller steps: Setting big goals can be overwhelming, but breaking them down into smaller, more manageable steps can make them feel more achievable. Create a plan of action with specific steps you can take to move closer to your goals.

– Practice gratitude: Take time each day to express gratitude for the blessings in your life, including the progress you've made toward your goals. This can help you stay positive and motivated, even when things get tough.

– Trust the process: Remember that achieving your goals is a journey, not a destination. Trust that everything is happening for a reason, and that you will learn and grow along the way. Have faith that you are exactly where you are meant to be, and that your higher power is guiding you toward your purpose.

Conclusion:

Incorporating faith into your goal-setting process can be a powerful way to achieve your dreams and find inner peace. Whether you're setting goals for your personal or professional life, having faith can help you stay focused, motivated, and positive. By starting with prayer or meditation, visualizing your goals, writing them down, breaking them down into smaller steps, practicing gratitude, and trusting the process, you can tap into the power of faith to achieve your goals.

It's important to remember that having faith doesn't mean that you won't encounter obstacles or setbacks along the way. In fact, it's often through these challenges that we grow and learn the most. But when you have faith, you can trust that everything is happening for a reason, and that you have the strength and guidance you need to overcome any obstacle.

If you're struggling to achieve your goals or feeling lost and directionless, try incorporating faith into your goal-setting process. Take some time to connect with your higher power, visualize your goals, write them down, and break them down into smaller steps. Practice gratitude for the progress you've made, and trust that everything is happening for a reason.

With faith, you can achieve anything you set your mind to. You have the power to overcome obstacles, achieve success, and find inner peace. So go ahead and set your goals, and trust that your higher power is guiding you every step of the way.

25: Overcoming Fear and Doubt through Faith

Introduction:

Fear and doubt are two of the most powerful emotions we can experience. They can hold us back from achieving our dreams, cause us to second-guess ourselves, and even prevent us from taking action altogether. But when we have faith, we can overcome fear and doubt and achieve anything we set our minds to. In this chapter, we'll explore the connection between faith and fear and doubt, and provide practical tips and strategies for using faith to overcome these powerful emotions.

Understanding Fear and Doubt:

Fear and doubt are natural emotions that everyone experiences from time to time. Fear is a response to a perceived threat, while doubt is a lack of confidence in ourselves or our abilities. While these emotions can be helpful in certain situations, such as when we need to protect ourselves from danger, they can also be harmful when they prevent us from taking action or pursuing our goals.

25: OVERCOMING FEAR AND DOUBT THROUGH FAITH

The problem with fear and doubt is that they can be paralyzing. When we're afraid or doubtful, we may hesitate to take action or make decisions, which can prevent us from moving forward in our personal or professional lives. We may second-guess ourselves, question our abilities, and ultimately give up on our dreams.

But when we have faith, we can overcome fear and doubt and achieve anything we set our minds to.

The Power of Faith:

Faith is a powerful force that can help us overcome fear and doubt. When we have faith, we believe that there is a higher power at work in the universe, guiding us toward our purpose and helping us overcome obstacles along the way. We trust that everything is happening for a reason, and that there is a higher purpose behind every challenge we face.

Having faith can give us the courage and strength we need to face our fears and overcome our doubts. It can help us stay focused and motivated, even when things get tough. And it can provide a sense of inner peace and fulfillment that can't be found through material possessions or external achievements.

25: OVERCOMING FEAR AND DOUBT THROUGH FAITH

So how can we use faith to overcome fear and doubt? Here are some practical tips and strategies:

– Identify the source of your fear or doubt: In order to overcome fear and doubt, we first need to understand where they're coming from. Are you afraid of failure? Are you doubtful of your abilities? Once you've identified the source of your fear or doubt, you can start to address it.

– Connect with your higher power: Take some time to connect with your higher power through prayer or meditation. Ask for guidance and support as you work to overcome your fears and doubts.

– Visualize success: Use your imagination to visualize yourself succeeding in the face of your fears and doubts. Imagine yourself achieving your goals, and feel the emotions that come with it. This can help you stay motivated and focused as you work to overcome your fears and doubts.

– Take action: Often, the best way to overcome fear and doubt is to take action. Even if you're afraid or doubtful, take a small step toward your goal. This can help build momentum and confidence, and make it easier to overcome your fears and doubts in the future.

– Practice gratitude: Take time each day to express gratitude for the blessings in your life, including the progress you've made in overcoming your fears and doubts. This can help you stay positive and motivated, even when things get tough.

– Surround yourself with positive influences: Surround yourself with people who support and encourage you, and who have faith in your abilities. This can help you stay motivated and focused, and provide a source of inspiration when you're feeling down.

Conclusion:

Fear and doubt are powerful emotions that can hold us back from achieving our dreams. But when we have faith, we can overcome these emotions and achieve anything we set our minds to. By identifying the source of our fears and doubts, connecting with our higher power, visualizing success, taking action, practicing gratitude, and surrounding ourselves with positive influences, we can tap into the power of faith and overcome even the biggest obstacles.

Remember, having faith doesn't mean that we'll never experience fear or doubt. It simply means that we trust that everything is happening for a reason, and that we have the strength and guidance we need to overcome any obstacle. With faith, we can achieve anything we set our minds to and live our best lives yet.

So if you're struggling with fear or doubt, take some time to connect with your higher power and trust that everything is happening for a reason. Visualize yourself succeeding in the face of your fears and doubts, and take small steps toward your goals, no matter how scary or uncertain they may seem. Practice gratitude for the progress you've made, and surround yourself with positive influences who will support and encourage you along the way.

With faith, anything is possible. So go ahead and take that first step toward your dreams, and trust that your higher power is guiding you every step of the way.

26: The Role of Faith in Creativity

Have you ever experienced a creative block? That feeling of being stuck, unable to come up with new ideas or inspiration, can be incredibly frustrating for anyone who relies on their creativity for work or personal fulfillment. But did you know that faith can play a powerful role in unlocking your creativity and helping you overcome creative blocks?

At its core, faith is about trusting in something greater than ourselves. It's about believing in a higher power, a purpose, or a mission that gives our lives meaning and direction. And when we apply this same faith to our creative endeavors, we can tap into a wellspring of inspiration and motivation that helps us create our best work.

One way that faith can help us tap into our creativity is by freeing us from the constraints of self-doubt and criticism. When we have faith in our abilities and our ideas, we're less likely to second-guess ourselves or worry about what others might think. Instead, we're free to explore new ideas and take risks, knowing that even if we fail, we're still on the right path and learning along the way.

Another way that faith can enhance our creativity is by helping us connect with our intuition and inner wisdom. When we trust in a higher power or purpose, we're more likely to listen to our inner voice and follow our instincts, rather than getting bogged down in logic or external pressures. This can lead to more authentic, original ideas that come from a place of deep personal conviction.

In addition, faith can provide a sense of purpose and meaning that can drive our creativity forward. When we believe that our work has a greater purpose, whether that's to inspire, educate, or entertain, we're more motivated to put in the effort and push through creative blocks. This can help us stay focused and committed to our creative projects, even when the going gets tough.

So how can we apply faith to our creative endeavors? Here are a few tips:

– Trust in your abilities and ideas. Have faith in yourself and your creative vision, and don't let self-doubt hold you back.

– Connect with your intuition. Take time to listen to your inner voice and follow your instincts, even if they don't make logical sense at first.

– Find meaning and purpose in your work. Identify the greater purpose behind your creative projects, and let that drive your motivation and commitment.

– Seek inspiration from a higher power. Whether that's through prayer, meditation, or connecting with nature, find ways to tap into a sense of awe and wonder that can fuel your creativity.

– Embrace risk-taking. Have faith that even if you fail, you're still on the right path and learning valuable lessons along the way.

In conclusion, faith can play a powerful role in unlocking our creativity and helping us overcome creative blocks. By trusting in ourselves, connecting with our intuition, finding meaning in our work, seeking inspiration from a higher power, and embracing risk-taking, we can tap into a wellspring of creativity and create our best work yet. So go ahead and have faith in your creative vision, and see where it takes you!

27: Faith and Personal Growth

Personal growth is a journey that we all embark on at some point in our lives. It's about becoming the best version of ourselves, learning from our experiences, and continually striving to improve in all areas of our lives. And when it comes to personal growth, faith can be a powerful tool to help us achieve our goals.

At its core, faith is about believing in something greater than ourselves. Whether that's a higher power, a purpose, or a mission, having faith gives us a sense of direction and purpose in life. And when we apply this same faith to our personal growth journey, we can tap into a wellspring of motivation, inspiration, and guidance that can help us achieve our goals and become the best version of ourselves.

Here are a few ways that faith can enhance our personal growth:

– Building resilience: Faith can help us build resilience in the face of adversity. When we believe that everything is happening for a reason and that there is a higher purpose to our struggles, we're more likely to bounce back from setbacks and keep moving forward.

– Developing self-awareness: Faith can also help us develop self-awareness. By reflecting on our beliefs and values, and connecting with our higher power, we can gain a deeper understanding of ourselves and our place in the world. This can help us identify areas for growth and make positive changes in our lives.

– Strengthening relationships: Faith can also play a role in strengthening our relationships with others. When we have faith in a higher power or purpose, we're more likely to treat others with kindness, compassion, and respect, and to seek out connections with like-minded individuals who share our values and beliefs.

– Cultivating gratitude: Gratitude is an essential component of personal growth, and faith can help us cultivate a sense of gratitude in our lives. When we believe that everything is a gift from our higher power, we're more likely to appreciate the good things in our lives and find meaning in even the smallest moments.

– Overcoming fear and doubt: Finally, faith can help us overcome fear and doubt. When we have faith in ourselves and our abilities, we're more likely to take risks and step outside our comfort zones. And when we encounter obstacles or setbacks, our faith can help us stay motivated and keep moving forward.

So how can we apply faith to our personal growth journey? Here are a few tips:

– Connect with your higher power: Whether that's through prayer, meditation, or other spiritual practices, make time to connect with your higher power and reflect on your beliefs and values.

– Reflect on your purpose: Take some time to reflect on your purpose and mission in life. What are your goals and aspirations? What do you hope to achieve in your personal growth journey?

– Practice gratitude: Cultivate a sense of gratitude in your life by focusing on the good things and expressing gratitude for the people and experiences that have shaped you.

– Seek out supportive relationships: Surround yourself with supportive relationships that encourage and inspire you, and seek out opportunities to connect with like-minded individuals who share your values and beliefs.

– Take risks: Finally, don't be afraid to take risks and step outside your comfort zone. Have faith in yourself and your abilities, and trust that everything is happening for a reason.

In conclusion, faith can be a powerful tool to enhance our personal growth journey. By building resilience, developing self-awareness, strengthening relationships, cultivating gratitude, and overcoming fear and doubt, we can tap into the power of faith and become the best version of ourselves. So go ahead and have faith in yourself and your journey, and see where it takes you!

28: The Role of Faith in Time Management

Time is a finite resource, and how we choose to spend it can have a significant impact on our lives. For many of us, time management is a constant struggle as we juggle multiple responsibilities and obligations. However, when we incorporate faith into our approach to time management, we can tap into a deeper sense of purpose and meaning that can help us prioritize our time and focus on what truly matters.

Here are a few ways that faith can enhance our time management:

– Setting priorities: Faith can help us set priorities in our lives based on our values and beliefs. When we have a clear understanding of what's most important to us, we can make better decisions about how to spend our time and focus on the things that matter most.

– Finding balance: Faith can also help us find balance in our lives. By taking time to connect with our higher power and reflect on our purpose, we can identify areas where we need to make adjustments and ensure that we're allocating our time in a way that aligns with our values and goals.

– Cultivating discipline: Time management requires discipline, and faith can help us cultivate the self-discipline necessary to make the most of our time. By staying focused on our purpose and connecting with our higher power, we can tap into a deeper sense of motivation and commitment that can help us stay on track and achieve our goals.

– Managing stress: Time management can be stressful, but faith can help us manage that stress. By focusing on our beliefs and connecting with our higher power, we can find a sense of peace and calm that can help us stay centered and focused even in the midst of a busy schedule.

– Building resilience: Finally, faith can help us build resilience in the face of challenges and setbacks. When we have faith in a higher purpose, we're more likely to bounce back from difficulties and keep moving forward even when things get tough.

So how can we incorporate faith into our approach to time management? Here are a few tips:

– Make time for reflection: Set aside time each day to reflect on your purpose and connect with your higher power. This can help you stay focused on what's most important and ensure that you're allocating your time in a way that aligns with your values and goals.

– Set priorities based on your values: Take some time to identify your values and beliefs and use them to set priorities in your life. This can help you make better decisions about how to spend your time and ensure that you're focusing on the things that matter most.

– Create a schedule: Create a schedule that allows you to allocate your time in a way that aligns with your priorities and goals. This can help you stay organized and ensure that you're making the most of your time.

– Practice self-discipline: Cultivate the self-discipline necessary to stick to your schedule and stay focused on your goals. This may involve saying "no" to certain obligations or making sacrifices in the short term to achieve your long-term goals.

– Find ways to manage stress: Identify strategies for managing stress, such as meditation, exercise, or prayer. By taking care of your mental and emotional well-being, you'll be better equipped to handle the challenges that come with time management.

In conclusion, faith can be a powerful tool to enhance our approach to time management. By setting priorities based on our values, finding balance, cultivating discipline, managing stress, and building resilience, we can tap into a deeper sense of purpose and meaning that can help us make the most of our time and achieve our goals. So go ahead and incorporate faith into your approach to time management, and see how it can transform your life!

29: Faith and Work-Life Balance

Introduction:

In today's fast-paced, demanding world, achieving a work-life balance can be a significant challenge. Many people struggle to manage their time effectively, and the pressures of work can spill over into their personal lives, leading to stress, burnout, and strained relationships. However, with the power of faith, it's possible to achieve a healthy balance between work and personal life, and experience greater fulfillment, joy, and peace in all areas of life.

The Importance of Work-Life Balance:

Achieving work-life balance is crucial for maintaining physical, mental, and emotional health. Chronic stress can have negative effects on both the mind and the body, leading to an increased risk of depression, anxiety, and physical illnesses. On the other hand, a healthy work-life balance can lead to increased happiness, improved relationships, and greater overall well-being.

The Role of Faith in Work-Life Balance:

Faith can be a powerful tool for achieving work-life balance.

By aligning your priorities with your values and living a life grounded in faith, you can experience a greater sense of purpose and meaning in both your personal and professional life. Faith can give you the strength and resilience to overcome obstacles, stay focused on your goals, and remain positive and hopeful, even in difficult circumstances.

Setting Priorities:

The first step to achieving work-life balance is setting priorities. This means identifying what's most important to you and making a plan to allocate your time and energy accordingly. For many people, family, health, and personal relationships are top priorities. However, it's also essential to dedicate time and attention to your career and professional growth.

Creating a Plan:

Once you've identified your priorities, the next step is to create a plan for achieving work-life balance. This might involve setting boundaries around work hours, delegating tasks to others, or finding ways to streamline your workflow. It's also important to schedule time for rest and renewal, as well as for activities that bring you joy and fulfillment outside of work.

Putting Faith into Action:

Putting your faith into action requires discipline, commitment, and a willingness to make sacrifices. You may need to set boundaries and say "no" to certain commitments in order to make time for your family, your health, and your personal life. You may need to restructure your work schedule or delegate some of your responsibilities to others. Whatever it takes, remember that your faith can give you the strength and perseverance to see it through.

Rest and Renewal:

One of the most important things you can do to maintain work-life balance is to set aside time for rest and renewal. This means taking breaks throughout the day to recharge your energy, as well as taking regular vacations and sabbaticals to give yourself time to rest, reflect, and rejuvenate. Whether it's spending time in nature, practicing meditation or mindfulness, or engaging in a hobby or creative pursuit, make sure to prioritize activities that bring you joy and fulfillment.

Building Healthy Relationships:

Another key aspect of work-life balance is cultivating healthy relationships. This includes building strong connections with your family, friends, and community, as well as nurturing positive relationships with your colleagues and clients. By investing in meaningful relationships, you can experience greater fulfillment and satisfaction in both your personal and professional life.

Conclusion:

In conclusion, faith plays a crucial role in achieving and maintaining work-life balance. By aligning your priorities with your values and committing to a plan that honors both your personal and professional responsibilities, you can live a fulfilling and balanced life. Through faith, you can find the strength, resilience, and inner peace to overcome obstacles and achieve success in all areas of your life.

30: Faith and Financial Planning

Introduction

Money plays a crucial role in our lives, and our financial stability is an essential part of our overall well-being. As such, it's crucial to have a solid financial plan in place, and faith can play a significant role in this regard. In this chapter, we will explore the role of faith in financial planning and how it can help you achieve your financial goals.

Faith and Money

Faith and money have been intertwined for centuries. Many religions have teachings and principles related to financial management and responsibility. For example, in Christianity, there are teachings on the importance of being good stewards of our resources, being content with what we have, and avoiding greed and materialism. Similarly, in Islam, there are principles related to giving to charity, being honest in financial dealings, and avoiding interest-based transactions.

The teachings of faith can provide a foundation for responsible financial management, regardless of your religious beliefs. By following these teachings, you can make wise financial decisions that align with your values, bring you peace of mind, and help you achieve your financial goals.

Setting Financial Goals

Faith can help you set financial goals that align with your values and beliefs. By examining your priorities and values, you can set goals that are meaningful to you and reflect your faith. For example, you may prioritize giving to charity, saving for your children's education, or supporting your community. By setting goals that align with your values, you can stay motivated and focused on achieving them.

Creating a Budget

Creating a budget is an essential part of financial planning, and faith can help you with this process. By examining your spending habits and priorities, you can create a budget that reflects your values and aligns with your financial goals. For example, you may want to allocate a certain percentage of your income to charitable giving or savings. By including these priorities in your budget, you can ensure that you're spending your money in a way that aligns with your values.

Dealing with Debt

Debt can be a significant source of stress and financial burden. Faith can help you deal with debt by providing principles related to financial responsibility and trust in a higher power. For example, in Christianity, there are teachings on the importance of avoiding debt and living within your means. Similarly, in Islam, there are principles related to avoiding interest-based transactions and being responsible with borrowed money.

By following these teachings, you can make wise decisions about borrowing and paying off debt. Additionally, faith can provide comfort and support during times of financial difficulty, helping you stay strong and maintain your sense of purpose and direction.

Investing and Planning for the Future

Investing and planning for the future are important parts of financial planning, and faith can help with these areas as well. By following principles of financial responsibility and wise investing, you can make choices that reflect your values and help you achieve your financial goals.

For example, you may choose to invest in socially responsible companies or avoid investments in industries that conflict with your values. Additionally, you may want to consider options like faith-based investment funds or financial advisors who specialize in working with people of faith.

Conclusion

Faith can play a significant role in financial planning, helping you set meaningful goals, make wise financial decisions, and stay focused on your priorities and values. By incorporating the principles of faith into your financial planning, you can achieve financial stability and security while maintaining a sense of purpose and direction in your life. Remember to seek guidance from trusted advisors and to pray for guidance and wisdom as you navigate the complex world of finance.

31: The Role of Faith in Success

Introduction:

Success is often defined as the achievement of a desired goal or outcome. Many of us have dreams and aspirations that we want to achieve, whether it's in our personal or professional lives. However, the road to success can be filled with obstacles, challenges, and setbacks that can test our perseverance and determination.

Faith is a powerful tool that can help us overcome these obstacles and achieve success. In this chapter, we will explore the role of faith in success and how it can transform our mindset, boost our confidence, and help us reach our full potential.

Faith and Mindset:

The first step in achieving success is developing the right mindset. Our mindset determines how we perceive the world around us and how we respond to challenges and setbacks. A positive mindset is essential for success, as it allows us to see opportunities where others see obstacles.

Faith can help us cultivate a positive mindset by providing

us with a sense of purpose and direction. When we have faith in a higher power or purpose, we can see beyond our current circumstances and focus on the bigger picture. This can help us stay motivated and focused, even in the face of adversity.

Faith and Confidence:

Confidence is another key component of success. When we believe in ourselves and our abilities, we are more likely to take risks, pursue our goals, and overcome obstacles. However, many of us struggle with self-doubt and insecurity, which can hold us back from reaching our full potential.

Faith can help us build confidence by reminding us of our inherent worth and value. When we have faith in a higher power or purpose, we can see ourselves as part of something bigger and more significant than our individual selves. This can help us overcome feelings of inadequacy and build confidence in our abilities and potential.

Faith and Resilience:

Resilience is the ability to bounce back from setbacks and challenges. It's an essential trait for success, as it allows us to persevere through difficult times and keep moving forward. However, building resilience can be challenging, especially when we're facing significant challenges or obstacles.

Faith can help us develop resilience by providing us with a sense of hope and purpose. When we have faith in a higher power or purpose, we can see beyond our current circumstances and focus on a brighter future. This can give us the strength and motivation to keep going, even when things get tough.

Faith and Action:

Finally, faith can help us take action towards our goals and dreams. Many of us have aspirations and desires that we want to achieve, but we may struggle with taking action or making progress. Faith can provide us with the courage and motivation to take bold steps towards our goals, even when we're afraid or uncertain.

When we have faith in a higher power or purpose, we can trust that our actions will lead us in the right direction. This can help us overcome our fears and doubts and take the necessary steps to achieve our goals and dreams.

Conclusion:

Faith is a powerful tool that can help us achieve success in all areas of our lives. By cultivating a positive mindset, building confidence, developing resilience, and taking bold action, we can overcome obstacles and reach our full potential. Whether we have faith in a higher power or purpose, or simply in ourselves and our abilities, we can tap into this powerful force to achieve our goals and live our best lives yet.

32: Faith and Gratitude

As mentioned earlier, gratitude is a powerful tool that can help us cultivate a positive mindset and improve our overall well-being. When we practice gratitude, we shift our focus from what we lack to what we have, and this can help us find greater joy and contentment in our lives. Furthermore, research has shown that people who regularly practice gratitude tend to experience lower levels of stress and depression, better sleep quality, and improved physical health.

So, how can faith help us cultivate gratitude? For many people, faith provides a framework for understanding and appreciating the blessings in their lives. Whether through prayer, meditation, or simply reflecting on the goodness of God, faith can help us connect with a sense of gratitude and thankfulness that transcends our circumstances.

One of the most powerful ways that faith can help us cultivate gratitude is by reminding us of the ultimate source of all good things. As the Bible says, "Every good and perfect gift is from above, coming down from the Father of the heavenly lights" (James 1:17). When we recognize that everything we have is a gift from God, it can help us approach life with a sense of humility and gratitude.

In addition to reminding us of the source of our blessings, faith can also help us find meaning and purpose in our lives. When we believe that we are part of a larger, divine plan, it can help us see the challenges and struggles of life in a different light. Rather than seeing them as obstacles to be overcome, we can view them as opportunities for growth and learning.

Moreover, faith can help us cultivate a sense of hope and optimism, even in the face of difficult circumstances. When we believe that God is working all things together for our good (Romans 8:28), we can approach life with a sense of trust and confidence, knowing that our future is in good hands.

Finally, faith can help us connect with others in a deeper and more meaningful way. When we recognize that all people are created in the image of God, it can help us see the inherent worth and value of each person, regardless of their background, beliefs, or circumstances. This can help us approach our relationships with greater empathy, kindness, and compassion, and it can help us find joy and fulfillment in serving others.

In conclusion, faith and gratitude are closely intertwined, and cultivating a sense of thankfulness can be a powerful way to deepen our faith and improve our overall well-being. Whether through prayer, meditation, or simply reflecting on the goodness of God, we can find countless reasons to be grateful, and we can trust that God will continue to bless us and guide us on our journey through life. So, let us approach each day with a sense of gratitude and trust, knowing that we are loved and valued by our Creator, and that He has a good and perfect plan for our lives.

33: Faith and Mindfulness

Faith and mindfulness are two concepts that might seem unrelated at first glance. Faith is often associated with religion and spirituality, while mindfulness is associated with meditation and being present in the moment. However, both faith and mindfulness share a common goal: to help us connect with ourselves and the world around us in a deeper, more meaningful way.

At its core, faith is about trusting in something greater than ourselves. It's about believing in a higher power, whether that be God, the universe, or some other force, that has a plan for our lives. Faith helps us find meaning and purpose in life, and it provides us with hope and comfort during times of struggle.

Similarly, mindfulness is about being present in the moment and paying attention to our thoughts, feelings, and surroundings without judgment. Mindfulness helps us become more aware of our thoughts and emotions, and it allows us to observe them without getting caught up in them. By practicing mindfulness, we can learn to control our reactions to stress and other negative emotions, which can lead to greater peace and happiness.

33: FAITH AND MINDFULNESS

So how do faith and mindfulness intersect? The answer lies in the practice of meditation. Meditation is a key component of both faith and mindfulness, and it can be used to enhance both practices.

In faith traditions, meditation is often used as a way to connect with God or a higher power. By quieting the mind and focusing on a specific prayer or mantra, we can enter into a state of deep reflection and contemplation. Through meditation, we can cultivate a sense of inner peace and tap into the wisdom and guidance of our faith.

Similarly, in mindfulness meditation, we focus on our breath or a particular sensation in order to become fully present in the moment. Through this practice, we can learn to observe our thoughts and emotions without judgment and to develop greater self-awareness. By cultivating mindfulness, we can become more attuned to our own needs and desires, and we can learn to respond to situations with greater clarity and compassion.

Together, faith and mindfulness can help us live a more balanced, meaningful, and fulfilling life. By incorporating both practices into our daily routines, we can develop a deeper connection with ourselves and the world around us. We can learn to approach life's challenges with greater resilience and equanimity, and we can cultivate a sense of gratitude and appreciation for all that life has to offer.

So whether you practice faith, mindfulness, or both, it's worth exploring how these two concepts can intersect and enhance each other. By taking time each day to meditate, reflect, and connect with something greater than ourselves, we can cultivate a greater sense of inner peace, purpose, and joy.

34: Faith and Meditation

Meditation is a powerful tool that has been used for thousands of years to help individuals find inner peace and clarity of mind. The practice of meditation involves training the mind to focus on a particular object or thought, allowing one to gain insight and understanding into the nature of the mind and the world around us.

The role of faith in meditation can be profound. By combining the practice of meditation with faith, individuals can deepen their connection with their spirituality and find greater peace and understanding in their lives. Faith can provide a sense of purpose and meaning that can help individuals stay committed to their meditation practice and find greater clarity and insight.

One of the ways in which faith can enhance meditation is by providing a framework for understanding the mind and the world around us. For example, many faith traditions emphasize the importance of compassion, forgiveness, and love. By focusing on these qualities during meditation, individuals can cultivate a greater sense of empathy and kindness towards themselves and others. This can help to reduce feelings of anger, anxiety, and depression and promote greater well-being and happiness.

In addition to providing a framework for understanding the mind and the world, faith can also help individuals find greater peace and acceptance in their lives. Many faith traditions emphasize the importance of surrendering to a higher power and trusting in the universe to guide our lives. By focusing on this idea during meditation, individuals can cultivate a greater sense of trust and surrender in their own lives, which can help to reduce feelings of stress and anxiety.

Furthermore, faith can help individuals find greater clarity and insight during meditation. Many faith traditions emphasize the importance of prayer and contemplation, which can help individuals to connect with their inner selves and gain greater insight into their thoughts and emotions. By incorporating prayer and contemplation into their meditation practice, individuals can deepen their understanding of themselves and the world around them.

The practice of meditation can also help individuals to deepen their faith. By quieting the mind and focusing on a particular object or thought, individuals can cultivate a greater sense of connection with their spirituality. This can help individuals to feel more connected to a higher power and gain greater clarity and insight into their spiritual path.

In addition to enhancing one's faith, the practice of meditation can also promote greater physical and mental health. Research has shown that regular meditation practice can help to reduce feelings of anxiety, depression, and stress, as well as improve sleep quality, lower blood pressure, and boost immune function. By incorporating faith into their meditation practice, individuals can enjoy even greater benefits for their physical and mental health.

Overall, the role of faith in meditation is a powerful one. By combining the practice of meditation with faith, individuals can deepen their connection with their spirituality, find greater peace and acceptance in their lives, and cultivate a greater sense of empathy, kindness, and understanding towards themselves and others. Whether one is new to meditation or has been practicing for years, the addition of faith can help to take their practice to new heights and unlock the full potential of this transformative tool.

35: Faith and Service

Faith and service are two concepts that are deeply intertwined. At its core, faith is about serving a higher power, whether that be God, the universe, or some other spiritual force. And as many religious and spiritual traditions teach, one of the best ways to serve that higher power is by serving others.

Service is not just about giving back to the community or helping those in need, although those are certainly important aspects of it. Service is also about cultivating an attitude of generosity, kindness, and compassion in our everyday lives. It is about recognizing that we are all interconnected, and that our actions have an impact on others.

When we approach service with a mindset of faith, we do so with the understanding that our actions are not just about doing good deeds for their own sake, but are also a reflection of our connection to something greater than ourselves. We recognize that by serving others, we are also serving our higher power.

In many faith traditions, service is seen as a way to demonstrate one's faith and to deepen one's spiritual practice. For example, in Christianity, Jesus is often cited as a model of service, and many churches and religious organizations emphasize the importance of volunteerism and community service. In Islam, one of the five pillars of the faith is zakat, or charitable giving, and Muslims are encouraged to give to those in need as a way to purify their wealth and show gratitude for their blessings.

But service is not just for those who adhere to a particular faith tradition. People from all backgrounds and beliefs can benefit from incorporating service into their lives. It can provide a sense of purpose and fulfillment, as well as a way to connect with others and build stronger communities.

Service can take many forms, from volunteering at a local food bank or homeless shelter, to donating time or resources to a cause we care about, to simply taking the time to listen to a friend or family member who is going through a difficult time. The key is to approach service with an open heart and a willingness to put the needs of others before our own.

When we serve others, we also benefit ourselves. Research has shown that acts of service can boost our mental health, improve our physical well-being, and even increase our lifespan. When we serve others, we also cultivate a sense of gratitude and humility, which can help us to live more fulfilling and meaningful lives.

Of course, it is important to remember that service is not about trying to earn points with our higher power or to boost our own egos. Rather, it is about recognizing our interconnectedness and using our gifts and talents to make the world a better place. As the writer and theologian Frederick Buechner once said, "The place God calls you to is the place where your deep gladness and the world's deep hunger meet."

In conclusion, faith and service are two concepts that are deeply intertwined, and both can play a powerful role in our personal and spiritual growth. By approaching service with a mindset of faith, we can cultivate an attitude of generosity, kindness, and compassion in our everyday lives, and demonstrate our connection to something greater than ourselves. Through service, we can not only make a difference in the world, but also deepen our own sense of purpose and meaning.

36: Conclusion: Living Your Best Life Through Faith

Congratulations! You have completed the journey through this comprehensive guide on faith. You have learned how to unlock the power of faith to overcome obstacles, achieve success, and find inner peace in your personal and professional life. You have transformed your mindset, boosted your confidence, and learned how to live your best life yet!

Throughout this book, we have explored various aspects of faith, including its role in overcoming fear, achieving success, improving relationships, enhancing mental and physical health, and finding meaning and purpose in life. We have also discussed practical strategies and techniques for developing and strengthening your faith, such as prayer, gratitude, mindfulness, meditation, and service.

By now, you should have a better understanding of how faith can help you navigate the ups and downs of life, and how you can incorporate faith into your daily routine to live a more fulfilling and purposeful life. However, it is important to remember that developing faith is an ongoing process that requires effort, commitment, and patience. Faith is not a one-time event, but a continuous journey of growth and transformation.

As you continue on your journey of faith, keep in mind these key takeaways:

– Faith is a powerful force that can help you overcome obstacles and achieve your goals, but it requires effort, patience, and persistence.

– Prayer, gratitude, mindfulness, meditation, and service are practical ways to develop and strengthen your faith.

– Living a life of faith involves aligning your thoughts, words, and actions with your values and beliefs.

– Your faith journey is unique to you, and you should not compare yourself to others or feel pressured to conform to certain expectations.

– Remember to be kind to yourself and others, and to seek support from your faith community or a trusted mentor when needed.

In conclusion, faith is an essential ingredient for living a fulfilling and purposeful life. By cultivating and nurturing your faith, you can tap into a power that can help you overcome any obstacle, achieve any goal, and find inner peace and joy. So, go forth with confidence, and may your faith continue to guide and inspire you on your journey towards living your best life yet!

Thank You

As we reach the end of this book, I want to say thanks for reading this book.

I want to get this information out to as many people as possible. If you found this book helpful, I would greatly appreciate you leaving me a review. This helps others find the book as well.

Disclaimer

This document is geared towards providing exact and reliable information in regards to the topic and issue covered. The publication is sold on the idea that the publisher is not required to render an accounting, officially permitted, or otherwise, qualified services. If advice is necessary, legal, financial, medical or professional, a practiced individual in the profession should be ordered.

This information is not presented by a financial or medical practitioner and is for entertainment, educational and informational purposes only. The content is not intended as a substitute for professional medical advice, diagnosis, or treatment. Always seek the advice of your physician or other qualified health care provider with any questions you may have regarding a medical condition. Never disregard professional medical advice or delay in seeking it because of something you have read.

The information provided herein is stated to be truthful and consistent, in that any liability, in terms of inattention or otherwise, by any usage or abuse of any policies, processes, or directions contained within is the solitary and utter responsibility of the recipient reader. Under no circumstances

DISCLAIMER

will any legal responsibility or blame be held against the publisher for any reparation, damages, or monetary loss due to the information herein, either directly or indirectly.

www.ingramcontent.com/pod-product-compliance
Lightning Source LLC
Chambersburg PA
CBHW060537130626
46553CB00002B/798